Gooseberry Patch co. ®

D0564500

# 101 *Autumn* RECIPES

Gooseberry Patch
2500 Farmers Dr., #110
Columbus, OH 43235

www.gooseberrypatch.com
1•800•854•6673

Copyright 2010, Gooseberry Patch 978-1-936283-09-5
Fourth Printing, May, 2011

# Gooseberry Patch
## *cookbooks*

Since 1992, we've been publishing our own country cookbooks for every kitchen and for every meal of the day! Each title has hundreds of budget-friendly recipes, using ingredients you already have on hand in your pantry.

In addition, you'll find helpful tips and ideas on every page, along with our hand-drawn artwork and plenty of personality. Their lay-flat binding makes them so easy to use...they're sure to become a fast favorite in your kitchen.

**Call us toll-free at**
# 1•800•854•6673
**and we'd be delighted to tell you all about our newest titles!**

**Shop with us online anytime at**
# www.gooseberrypatch.com

## Send us your favorite recipe!

*and the memory that makes it special for you!*\* If we select your recipe for a brand-new **Gooseberry Patch** cookbook, your name will appear right along with it...and you'll receive a FREE copy of the book!

Submit your recipe on our website at
**www.gooseberrypatch.com**

Or mail to:

**Gooseberry Patch** • Attn: Cookbook Dept.
2500 Farmers Dr., #110 • Columbus, OH 43235

*\*Please include the number of servings and all other necessary information!*

## Have a taste for more?

Visit **www.gooseberrypatch.com** to join our **Circle of Friends**!

- Free recipes, tips and ideas plus a complete cookbook index
- Get special email offers and our monthly eLetter delivered to your inbox
- Find local stores with **Gooseberry Patch** cookbooks, calendars and organizers

# CONTENTS

School Days............................ 7

Busy-Day Dinners.................. 32

Fun with Friends ................... 58

Country Harvest .................... 82

# Dedication

To everyone who delights
in the friendship,
festivity and food
that autumn brings!

# Appreciation

We give thanks to you,
our friends, who shared
your tastiest recipes
of the season!

# Bran & Raisin Muffins

2 c. bran and raisin cereal
1-1/2 c. milk
1-1/2 c. all-purpose flour
1 t. baking soda
1/4 t. salt
1 egg, beaten
1/2 c. brown sugar, packed
2 T. butter, melted

Mix cereal with milk; set aside.
In a large bowl, combine remaining
ingredients; stir in cereal mixture.
Fill lightly greased or paper-lined
muffin cups about 2/3 full with
batter. Bake at 350 degrees for
20 to 25 minutes. Makes one dozen.

7

Jody Pressley
Charlotte, NC

Filled with plump raisins,
these sweet muffins are
perfect for breakfast or
tucked into a lunch box.

# Break-of-Day Smoothie

15-1/4 oz. can fruit cocktail
8-oz. container vanilla yogurt
1 c. pineapple juice
6 to 8 ice cubes
Optional: 3 to 4 T. wheat germ

Combine all ingredients in a blender.
Blend until smooth. Serves 2.

Cheri Maxwell
Gulf Breeze, FL

Make this just the way
you like it, using your
favorite flavors of yogurt
and fruit.

# Breakfast Burritos

16-oz. pkg. ground pork
    sausage
8-oz. pkg. shredded
    Mexican-blend cheese
10-oz. can diced tomatoes
    with chiles
5 eggs, beaten
8  10-inch flour tortillas

Brown sausage in a skillet; drain.
In a bowl, combine sausage, cheese
and tomatoes. Cook eggs in the
skillet. Add eggs to sausage mixture
and mix thoroughly. Divide mixture
evenly among tortillas and roll
tightly. Seal tortillas by cooking for
one to 2 minutes on a hot griddle
sprayed with non-stick vegetable
spray. Makes 8 servings.

9

Cherie White
Oklahoma City, OK

Freeze a batch of these
tasty burritos. Then for
breakfast, just pop into
the microwave for two
minutes and enjoy.

# My Mom's Muffin Doughnuts

2 c. all-purpose flour
1/2 t. salt
1 T. baking powder
1/2 t. nutmeg
1/2 c. plus 1/2 t. margarine,
   divided
1-1/2 c. sugar, divided
1 egg, beaten
3/4 c. milk
3/4 c. semi-sweet chocolate chips
1/2 c. chopped pecans
2 t. cinnamon

Combine flour, salt, baking powder, nutmeg, 1/2 teaspoon margarine, 1/2 cup sugar, egg and milk. Fold in chocolate chips and pecans. Fill greased muffin cups 2/3 full. Bake at 350 degrees for 20 minutes. Remove immediately from pan. Melt the remaining butter; roll muffins in butter. Combine remaining sugar and cinnamon; roll muffins in mixture. Makes one dozen.

Laura Parker
Flagstaff, AZ

My mom made these often!
It was always fun to find
them stacked on a plate.
I still enjoy making them
for my adult daughters!

# Baked Pancakes with Sausage

1-3/4 c. all-purpose flour
4 t. baking powder
5 t. sugar
1 t. salt
3 eggs
1-1/2 c. milk
3 T. margarine, melted
1 lb. pork sausage breakfast links,
    browned and drained
Garnish: butter, warm syrup

11

Mix together flour, baking powder, sugar and salt; set aside. In a large bowl, beat eggs until fluffy; mix in milk and margarine. Gradually stir in flour mixture until smooth. Pour batter into a greased 15"x10" jelly-roll pan. Arrange sausages on top of batter. Bake at 450 degrees for 15 minutes, or until pancakes are done. Cut into squares and serve with butter and syrup. Makes 8 to 10 servings.

Jill Velentine
Jackson, TN
I cook up the sausage and mix the dry ingredients the night before to save time in the morning!

# Overnight Cherry Oatmeal

3 c. long-cooking oats, uncooked
3/4 c. powdered sugar
1/4 t. salt
21-oz. can cherry pie filling
6 c. water
1 t. almond extract

Combine oats, powdered sugar and salt in a large bowl; pour into a slow cooker that has been sprayed with non-stick vegetable spray. Add remaining ingredients; stir until combined. Cover and cook on low setting for 8 hours. Serves 4 to 6.

Lynda Robson
Boston, MA

Assemble the night before and wake to the aroma of cherry pie...what a way to start the day!

# Kids' Favorite Fruit Salad

14-1/2 oz. can peach pie filling
1 c. pineapple, peeled and diced
1 c. seedless red grapes
2 bananas, sliced
11-oz. can mandarin oranges,
    drained
1 c. mini marshmallows

Mix all ingredients together in a large
bowl and refrigerate until chilled.
Serves 6 to 8.

13

Carrie Fostor
Baltic, OH

This simple recipe will have
the kids asking for more!
Great for picnics, potlucks
and school lunches. I keep
it on hand for snacks!

# Cinnamon Toast Balls

12 slices bread, crusts removed
1/4 c. butter, melted
1 T. cinnamon
1 T. sugar

Tear each slice of bread in half. Roll each half into a ball and place on an ungreased baking sheet. Drizzle balls with melted butter. Combine cinnamon and sugar and sprinkle over balls. Bake at 350 degrees for 5 to 7 minutes. If desired, broil until lightly golden, about 2 minutes. Makes 2 dozen.

Martha Stephens
Sibley, LA

I'm always looking for something creative for my kids to eat. Instead of traditional cinnamon toast, I make these!

# Good-for-You Snack

6 c. doughnut-shaped oat cereal
1 c. salted peanuts
1 c. raisins
1 c. brown sugar, packed
1/2 c. butter, softened
1/4 c. corn syrup
1/2 t. salt
1/2 t. baking soda

Combine cereal, peanuts and raisins in a buttered large mixing bowl; set aside. Cook brown sugar, butter, corn syrup and salt in a saucepan over medium heat, stirring constantly until bubbly around the edges. Boil for 2 minutes, stirring occasionally. Remove from heat; stir in baking soda. Pour over cereal mixture; stir until well coated. Divide and spread evenly into 2 greased 13"x9" baking pans. Bake at 250 degrees for 15 minutes. Stir; let cool for 10 minutes. Loosen sides with a spatula; cool until firm, about 30 minutes. Break into bite-size pieces; store in an airtight container. Makes about 20 servings.

15

Mickey Scheive
Highland, IN
Makes an ideal snack for the kids to munch on between classes.

# Cheese Pops

2  3-oz. pkgs. cream cheese,
   softened
2 c. finely shredded Cheddar
   cheese
1-1/2 c. carrots, peeled and finely
   shredded
2 t. honey
1 c. pecans, finely chopped
4 doz. pretzel sticks

Combine cheeses, carrots and honey;
chill for one hour. Shape into one-inch
balls and then roll in pecans. Chill,
then insert pretzel sticks before serving.
Makes 3 to 4 dozen.

Carol Hickman
Kingsport, TN

Instead of serving one
large cheese ball, consider
making these...the right
size for little hands!

# A Pocket Full of Pizza

1 c. shredded mozzarella cheese
1/2 c. pizza sauce
2  6-inch pita rounds, halved
1/3 c. sliced mushrooms
1/3 c. red or green pepper,
    sliced
1/3 c. broccoli, chopped

Combine cheese and sauce. Spoon
1/4 cup cheese mixture inside each
pita; add vegetables. Wrap each pita
in aluminum foil and seal closed.
Place on an ungreased baking sheet.
Bake at 375 degrees for 8 to
10 minutes. Let cool several minutes
before serving. Serves 4.

17

### Maria Masi
### Mansfield, OH

Add any vegetable or
pizza fixings you like
to these pockets!

# Mini Turkey-Berry Bites

2 c. biscuit baking mix
1/2 c. sweetened dried cranberries
1 c. milk
2 T. Dijon mustard
1 egg, beaten
6-oz. pkg. thinly sliced smoked
    turkey, chopped and divided
3/4 c. shredded Swiss cheese,
    divided

Stir together baking mix, cranberries, milk, mustard and egg until blended. Pour half the batter into a lightly greased 8"x8" baking pan. Arrange half the turkey over batter; sprinkle half the cheese nearly to edges of pan. Top with remaining turkey, followed by remaining batter. Bake, uncovered, at 350 degrees for 45 to 50 minutes, until golden and set. Sprinkle with remaining cheese; let stand 5 minutes. To serve, cut into 9 squares; slice each square diagonally. Makes 1-1/2 dozen.

Jackie Smulski
Lyons, IL

Everybody will gobble
these hearty "sandwiches"
right up!

# ABC Chicken Soup

1 onion, chopped
2 carrots, peeled and chopped
2 stalks celery, chopped
1 T. oil
2 cloves garlic, minced
2  32-oz. containers chicken
   broth
2 c. cooked chicken, shredded
1/4 t. dried thyme
salt and pepper to taste
1/2 c. alphabet-shaped pasta,
   uncooked

In a Dutch oven over medium-high heat, sauté onion, carrots and celery in hot oil for 5 minutes. Add garlic and sauté one minute. Stir in broth, chicken and seasonings. Bring to a boil. Reduce heat and simmer 15 minutes, stirring occasionally. Add pasta and cook 8 minutes, until tender. Serves 8 to 10.

Regina Vining
Warwick, RI

My kids are so busy spelling their names in this soup, they don't realize they're eating veggies!

# Quick Lunchbox Cake

2-1/4 c. all-purpose flour
2 t. baking soda
1 t. salt
1 c. brown sugar, packed
2 eggs, beaten
1/4 c. butter, softened
1 c. fruit cocktail, drained
1/2 c. semi-sweet chocolate chips
1/2 c. chopped nuts

Combine all ingredients except chocolate chips and nuts. Blend well with an electric hand mixer on low speed. Pour batter into a greased and floured 13"x9" baking pan. Sprinkle chips and nuts over batter. Bake at 350 degrees for 35 to 40 minutes. Cool and cut into squares. Makes 16 servings.

**Judy Fingerson**
**Auburn, WA**

My mother made this when we were kids in the 50s. It's not messy and easy to handle. It really does go well in a lunchbox!

# PB & Berries

1 T. creamy peanut butter
3 slices whole-wheat bread
1 T. whipped cream cheese
2 strawberries, hulled and sliced
1 t. honey

Spread peanut butter on one slice of bread; arrange strawberries on top and drizzle with honey. Place a plain piece of bread on top of peanut butter slice. Spread cream cheese on remaining slice of bread and place on top. Cut into halves. Makes 2 servings.

21

Jo Ann
This sandwich takes plain PB & J to new heights! Toast the bread for a warm and gooey treat.

# Oven-Fried Chips

Claire Bertram
Lexington, KY

Use an adjustable cheese slicer or food processor to slice the potatoes as thinly as possible...they'll get nice and crunchy!

1/4 c. olive oil, divided
1 sweet potato, peeled and
    thinly sliced
1 potato, thinly sliced
1/2 t. dried rosemary
1 t. lemon zest
1 t. kosher salt
1/2 t. pepper
1/4 t. cinnamon
1/8 t. nutmeg
1/8 t. ground ginger
1 t. orange zest
1 t. sugar

Grease 2 baking sheets with a teaspoon each of olive oil. In single layers, arrange sweet potato slices on one sheet; arrange white potato slices on the other. Use a pastry brush and remaining olive oil to lightly coat top of each potato slice. Bake at 400 degrees until golden and crisp, about 10 minutes. Drain on paper towels. Combine rosemary, lemon zest, salt and pepper. In another bowl, combine remaining ingredients. While still warm, sprinkle sweet potato chips with cinnamon mixture; sprinkle white potato chips with rosemary mixture. Makes 4 servings.

# Baked Quesadillas

2 8-oz. cans chicken, drained
  and flaked
1 to 2 T. taco seasoning mix
8-oz. jar salsa
8-oz. pkg. shredded
  Mexican-blend cheese
16 8-inch flour tortillas
Garnish: sour cream, avocado
  slices

23

Mix chicken, taco seasoning, salsa
and cheese. Arrange 8 tortillas on
baking sheets sprayed with non-stick
vegetable spray. Spread chicken
mixture onto tortillas. Top with
remaining tortillas. Spray tops with
non-stick vegetable spray. Bake at
350 degrees for 5 to 10 minutes,
until tops are golden. Allow to cool
for a few minutes; cut into quarters.
Garnish with sour cream and avocado
slices. Makes 8 servings.

Patti Walker
Mocksville, NC

Quesadillas are a nice
change from tacos. Sometimes
we make these only with
cheese. My children enjoy
them as a meal or as
a quick snack.

# Warm Spiced Milk

2-1/2 c. milk
1/3 c. apple butter
2-1/2 T. maple syrup
1/4 t. cinnamon
1/8 t. ground cloves

Whisk ingredients together in a heavy saucepan. Heat over low heat until milk steams (do not boil). Makes 4 servings.

Loni Ventura
Wimauma, FL

A tummy-warming beverage... tastes like a baked apple in a mug!

# After-School Doughnuts

2 c. buttermilk
3 eggs, beaten
1/3 c. shortening
2 t. salt
1 t. baking soda
1 t. nutmeg
1/2 t. cinnamon
2 c. sugar
5 c. all-purpose flour, divided
oil for deep frying

Blend buttermilk, eggs and shortening together in a large bowl; set aside. In a separate bowl, sift together salt, baking soda, nutmeg, cinnamon, sugar and 2 cups flour; add to buttermilk mixture. Stir in remaining flour; cover and refrigerate overnight. Roll out on a lightly floured surface to 1/3-inch thickness; cut into 3-inch rounds. Heat 3 inches of oil in a heavy stockpot over medium-high heat to 375 degrees. Add doughnuts a few at a time, cooking until golden on both sides, about 2 minutes. Drain on paper towels. Makes 4 to 5 dozen.

25

Stacey Weichert
Moorhead, MN

While I was growing up, Mom made doughnuts when cold days rolled around. Whenever I came home from school, the house would be filled with the aroma of cinnamon.

# Chicken Nuggets

2-1/2 c. corn flake cereal,
   crushed
1 t. paprika
1/2 t. garlic powder
1/2 t. dried oregano
1 egg white
1 lb. boneless, skinless chicken
   breasts, cut into 1-inch cubes
Garnish: honey, mustard, catsup

In a plastic zipping bag, combine cereal and seasonings; shake to mix. Place egg white in a shallow bowl and beat slightly. Working with 6 pieces at a time, dip chicken in egg; add to bag and shake to coat. Bake at 425 degrees on a greased baking sheet until crisp, about 15 to 20 minutes. Serve with honey, mustard and catsup for dipping. Serves 4.

Janice Ertola
Martinez, CA

For an Italian twist, add 1/3 cup of grated Parmesan cheese to the cereal mixture and serve with warm spaghetti sauce.

# Mac & Cheese Cupcakes

8-oz. pkg. elbow macaroni,
   cooked
1 t. olive oil
1-1/2 c. milk
2 T. cornstarch
1 t. Dijon mustard
salt and pepper to taste
2 c. shredded sharp Cheddar
   cheese
1/2 c. seasoned dry bread crumbs

Toss macaroni with olive oil; set aside. In a medium saucepan, whisk milk and cornstarch until blended. Bring to a boil over medium heat, stirring often. Stir in mustard, salt and pepper. Reduce heat and simmer until thickened, stirring frequently. Add cheese and stir until melted; fold in macaroni. Grease 12 muffin cups with butter, coat with bread crumbs and shake off excess. Spoon in macaroni mixture. Bake at 350 degrees for 15 to 25 minutes, until golden. Makes one dozen.

27

Shelley Turner
Boise, ID
I like to make these on the weekends and then pop them in the microwave when I see the kids get off the bus.

# Ranch Ham & Tortilla Pinwheels

2  8-oz. pkgs. cream cheese,
    softened
.4-oz. pkg. ranch salad dressing
    mix
2 green onions, minced
4  12-inch flour tortillas
1/4 lb. sliced deli ham
4-oz. can diced green chiles,
    drained
Optional: 2-1/4 oz. can sliced
    black olives, drained
Garnish: salsa

Mix together cream cheese, dressing
mix and green onions; spread on
tortillas. Layer with ham and sprinkle
with chiles and olives, if using. Roll
tortillas tightly. Chill for at least
2 hours, or overnight. Slice rolls into
one-inch pieces and serve with salsa.
Makes 3 dozen.

Lisa Johnson
Hallsville, TX
These are a favorite of all
ages...after school, after
work or just because!

# Raisin-Filled Cookies

1 c. shortening
1 c. sugar
1 c. brown sugar, packed
3 eggs, beaten
4 c. all-purpose flour
1 t. baking soda
1/2 t. salt
1 t. vanilla extract

Mix together all ingredients until well combined. Roll out on a lightly floured surface to 1/4-inch thick. Cut out with a 2-inch round cookie cutter. Spread Raisin Filling onto half the cookies. Arrange remaining cookies over filling; press edges with a fork dipped in flour to seal. Place on greased baking sheets. Bake at 350 degrees for 9 to 10 minutes. Makes 1-1/2 to 2 dozen.

**Raisin Filling:**

1 c. raisins, finely chopped
1/2 c. water
1 T. sugar
1 T. all-purpose flour

Mix together all ingredients in a saucepan over medium heat. Bring to a boil. Remove from heat; cool slightly.

29

Barbara Schmeckpeper
Minooka, IL

My grandma did so many special things. She always served hot chocolate to us grandchildren along with these delicious cookies. What fond memories!

# Cale's Corn Flake Cookies

1 c. light corn syrup
1 c. creamy peanut butter
1 c. sugar
1 t. vanilla extract
6 to 7 c. corn flake cereal

Combine all ingredients except cereal in a heavy saucepan; cook and stir over low heat. Add cereal; stir well and drop by tablespoonfuls onto wax paper. Let stand until set. Makes 4 dozen.

Lori Hobscheidt
Washington, IA

Sweet, crunchy and peanut buttery. An easy cookie recipe using pantry staples!

# Ravioli Taco Bake

1-1/2 lbs. ground beef
1-1/4 oz. pkg. taco seasoning mix
3/4 c. water
40-oz. can meat-filled ravioli
   with sauce
8-oz. pkg. shredded Cheddar
   cheese
Optional: sliced black olives

Brown ground beef in a large skillet over medium heat; drain. Stir in seasoning mix and water. Reduce heat; simmer for 8 to 10 minutes. Place ravioli in a lightly greased 13"x9" baking pan; spoon beef mixture over top. Sprinkle with cheese. Bake, uncovered, at 350 degrees for 25 to 30 minutes, until cheese is melted and bubbly. If desired, sprinkle with olives before serving. Serves 6 to 8.

31

Margie Kirkman
High Point, NC

So easy! Tasty as a weeknight meal or in a lunchbox thermos.

# Red Pepper Muffins

1/2 c. butter
1/2 c. red pepper, finely chopped
Optional: 1/3 c. green onions,
  finely chopped
2 eggs, beaten
2/3 c. sour cream
1-1/2 c. all-purpose flour
2 T. sugar
1-1/2 t. baking powder
1/4 t. baking soda
3/4 t. salt
1/2 t. dried basil
1/4 t. dried tarragon

Melt butter in a skillet over medium heat. Cook pepper and onions until tender; let cool. In a bowl, mix eggs and sour cream; stir in pepper mixture. In a separate bowl, combine remaining ingredients. Stir in egg mixture until just moistened. Fill 10 greased muffin cups 2/3 full. Bake at 350 degrees for 20 to 25 minutes, until a toothpick tests clean. Serve warm. Makes 10 muffins.

Marian Buckley
Fontana, CA

My husband likes making breakfast for supper... I'll bake these while he scrambles the eggs!

# Slow-Cooker Sweet Potato Chili

28-oz. can diced tomatoes
16-oz. can black beans, drained
   and rinsed
16-oz. can kidney beans, drained
   and rinsed
1 onion, chopped
1 red pepper, chopped
1 green pepper, chopped
3 to 4 stalks celery, chopped
2 sweet potatoes, peeled and cut
   into 1/2-inch cubes
Optional: 1 lb. ground beef
   or ground turkey, browned
   and drained; canned diced
   jalapeños or hot pepper
   sauce to taste
8-oz. pkg. shredded
   Mexican-blend or
   Cheddar cheese

Combine all ingredients except
cheese in a slow cooker; stir to mix.
Cover and cook on low setting
8 to 10 hours, or on high setting
4 to 5 hours. Garnish with cheese.
Serves 6.

33

Cheryl Fernstrom
Exeter, RI
The vegetables cook up
nice and bright! A tasty
warm-you-up meal on a
cold and windy day.

# Parmesan Zucchini Sticks

1 egg
1/2 c. Italian-flavored dry bread
  crumbs
1/2 c. grated Parmesan cheese
1 t. dried thyme
1/2 t. pepper
4 zucchini, quartered lengthwise
Garnish: ranch salad dressing

Whisk egg in a shallow bowl; set aside.
Mix bread crumbs, cheese, thyme and
pepper in a separate bowl. Dip zucchini
into egg and then into crumb mixture.
Place on a baking sheet sprayed with
non-stick vegetable spray. Bake at
450 degrees for 20 to 25 minutes, until
tender. Serve with ranch salad dressing
or your favorite dipping sauce. Serves 4.

Marion Sundberg
Ramona, CA

Instead of French fries,
serve these alongside
cheeseburgers...kids will
gobble them up!

# Thumbs-Up Cornbread Salad

8-1/2 oz. pkg. cornbread mix
24-oz. can pinto beans, drained
   and rinsed
2  15-oz. cans corn, drained
1/4 c. sweet onion, diced
1 c. cherry tomatoes, quartered
1/3 c. celery, chopped
1/2 c. bacon bits, divided
2 c. shredded 4-cheese blend
   cheese, divided
1 c. sour cream
2 c. ranch salad dressing

Prepare and bake cornbread according to package directions; set aside to cool. Crumble cornbread into a large serving bowl. Add beans, corn, onion, tomatoes, celery, 1/4 cup bacon bits and 1-1/2 cups cheese. Toss well; set aside. In another bowl, mix sour cream and salad dressing together; drizzle over cornbread mixture and toss to coat. Sprinkle with remaining bacon bits and cheese. Serves 10.

Jana Timmons
Hendersonville, TN

Be sure to get your share early...it'll be gone before you know it!

# Kielbasa Mac & Cheese

7-oz. pkg. macaroni & cheese mix
1 lb. Kielbasa sausage, sliced
10-3/4 oz. can cream of
   chicken soup
1/3 c. milk
2 c. shredded Cheddar cheese,
   divided
Optional: dried parsley or cayenne
   pepper to taste

Prepare macaroni & cheese according
to package directions. In a large bowl,
combine sausage, prepared macaroni
& cheese, soup, milk and one cup
Cheddar cheese. Mix well; pour into
a greased 1-1/2 quart casserole dish.
Top with remaining cheese and
sprinkle with parsley or cayenne
pepper, if desired. Bake, uncovered,
at 350 degrees for about 30 minutes,
or until heated through. Serves 4 to 6.

Tammy Rogers
Gordonsville, VA

So easy to make...whip it
up for any weeknight
dinner. If you don't have
Kielbasa, try hot dogs!

# ABC Salad

1/2 c. canola oil
1/4 c. lemon juice, divided
1 t. sugar
1/4 t. salt
1 c. sweetened dried cranberries
3 red apples, cored and cut into
    1/2-inch cubes
2 c. broccoli flowerets
1/2 c. chopped walnuts

In a bowl, whisk together oil,
2 tablespoons lemon juice, sugar
and salt. Add cranberries; let stand
for 10 minutes. In a large bowl, toss
apples with remaining lemon juice.
Add broccoli, walnuts and cranberry
mixture; toss to coat. Cover and
refrigerate for 2 hours, or until
chilled. Toss before serving. Makes
6 to 8 servings.

37

**Karen Keenan**
**Worthington, OH**

ABC stands for apples,
broccoli and cranberries.
Crisp and fresh...just like
a fall breeze!

# Bowtie Pasta & Veggies

2 T. oil
16-oz. pkg. frozen mixed bell
   peppers, thawed
1 yellow squash, diced
1 zucchini, diced
8-oz. pkg. bowtie pasta, cooked
1/4 t. garlic, minced
1/2 t. salt
1/2 c. shredded mozzarella cheese
1/2 c. shredded provolone cheese
1/2 c. shredded Parmesan cheese

Heat oil in a large saucepan over medium heat; sauté vegetables together until lightly golden and tender. Stir in cooked pasta, garlic and salt. Sprinkle with cheeses and stir until melted. Serves 4 to 6.

Margaret Phares
Jackson Center, PA

This makes a great meal all on its own...sometimes I serve it topped with grilled chicken.

# Oh-So-Easy Peach Cobbler

2 15-oz. cans sliced peaches,
   drained and 1/2 c. juice
   reserved
1/2 c. butter, sliced
1 c. self-rising flour
1 c. sugar
1 c. milk

Arrange peaches in a 13"x9" baking pan that has been sprayed with non-stick vegetable spray. Pour in reserved juice. Place butter slices over peaches. In a bowl, mix flour, sugar and milk, stirring until smooth. Pour over peaches, spreading batter to the edges of pan. Bake at 375 degrees for 30 minutes, or until golden. Serves 10 to 12.

39

Dueley Lucas
Somerset, KY

Wonderful by itself
or topped with milk or
vanilla ice cream.

# Slow-Simmered Baked Beans

2  14-oz. cans pinto beans,
   drained and rinsed
2  14-oz. cans navy beans, drained
   and rinsed
28-oz. can vegetarian baked beans
7-oz. can diced green chiles
1-1/2 c. catsup
1/2 c. brown sugar, packed
3 T. rice vinegar
1 t. smoke-flavored cooking sauce
1 onion, chopped
1 red pepper, chopped
1 lb. bacon, crisply cooked and
   chopped

Combine all ingredients in a slow
cooker. Cover and cook on low setting
for 6 to 8 hours, or on high setting for
4 hours. Makes 10 to 12 servings.

Kerry Hoyle
Pollock Pines, CA

This dish always
seems to show up at
family gatherings!

# Cheesy Chicken & Noodles

12-oz. pkg. wide egg noodles,
  cooked
2 c. cooked chicken, cubed
  or shredded
2  10-3/4 oz. cans chicken
  noodle soup
10-3/4 oz. can cream of
  chicken soup
2 eggs, beaten
2 c. shredded Cheddar cheese
1 c. seasoned dry bread crumbs
1 t. garlic salt
1 t. onion salt
salt and pepper to taste

Combine all ingredients in a
large bowl; mix well. Transfer to a
lightly greased 13"x9" baking pan.
Bake, uncovered, at 350 degrees for
35 to 40 minutes. Serves 8 to 10.

41

April Bash
Carlisle, PA

This was given to me by my
dearest aunt and I have
tweaked it a little for
my family's liking. It is
so cheesy and delicious.

# Hamburger Crunch

2 lbs. ground beef
1 T. onion, minced
2  10-3/4 oz. cans tomato soup
1 t. chili powder
4 c. corn chips
8-oz. pkg. shredded Cheddar
   cheese

Brown ground beef and onion together
in a large skillet over medium heat;
drain. Stir in soup and chili powder.
Spread in an ungreased 13"x9" baking
pan; top with corn chips. Bake,
uncovered, at 350 degrees for 20 to
25 minutes. Remove from oven;
sprinkle with cheese. Bake for an
additional 5 minutes, until cheese
melts. Serves 6 to 8.

Gayle Ortmeyer
Jefferson City, MO

If you have any
leftovers, roll them up
in flour tortillas for
tasty burritos.

# Carol's Creamy Tomato Soup

4 tomatoes, peeled and diced
4 c. tomato juice
1/4 c. fresh basil
1 c. whipping cream
1/2 c. butter
salt and pepper to taste

In a stockpot over medium-low heat, simmer tomatoes and juice for 30 minutes. Purée tomato mixture and basil in a food processor; return to pot. Stir in remaining ingredients. Cook over low heat, stirring until butter is melted; do not boil. Garnish with Grilled Cheese Croutons. Serves 4.

**Grilled Cheese Croutons:**

1/4 c. butter, softened
1/4 t. dried thyme
6 slices bread
3 slices American cheese

Combine butter and thyme; spread over one side of each bread slice. Place 3 slices in a skillet, buttered-side down. Top each with a cheese slice and a bread slice, buttered-side up. Cook over medium-high heat for 3 to 5 minutes per side, until toasted and golden. Cut into one-inch squares.

43

Tori Willis
Champaign, IL

My Aunt Carol taught me the grilled-cheese crouton trick...sometimes I use Cheddar cheese and wheat bread.

# Pork Chops with Apple Stuffing

1 T. olive oil
3 T. butter, divided
5 boneless pork chops
1 apple, cored and chopped
1/2 c. onion, chopped
1-2/3 c. water
6-oz. pkg. stuffing mix

Heat oil and one tablespoon butter in a large skillet over medium heat. Add pork chops; cook for 8 to 10 minutes, turning once, until cooked through. Remove chops; cover to keep warm. Melt remaining butter in skillet; add apple and onion. Cook for 3 to 5 minutes, stirring occasionally, until tender. Add water; bring to a boil. Stir in stuffing mix; remove from heat. Arrange chops over stuffing mixture; cover and let stand for 5 minutes before serving. Serves 5.

Sherry Lamb Noble
Kennett, MO

This tastes so good with a side of steamed green beans.

# No-Bake Pumpkin-Butterscotch Pie

8-oz. container frozen whipped topping, thawed
1 c. canned pumpkin
3.4-oz. pkg. instant butterscotch pudding mix
1/4 c. brown sugar, packed
1 t. pumpkin pie spice
2 T. brewed coffee, cooled
9-inch graham cracker crust

Stir together whipped topping, pumpkin and dry pudding mix. Add brown sugar, spice and coffee; stir briskly for 2 minutes. Spoon mixture into crust. Cover and refrigerate for at least 2 hours before serving. Serves 6 to 8.

45

**Andrea Heyart**
**Aubrey, TX**

I whipped up this dessert in a hurry when some unexpected company visited. It was delicious...they request it every time now!

# Italian Chicken Pie

3/4 c. cottage cheese
1/3 c. grated Parmesan cheese
1-1/2 c. cooked chicken, cubed
1-1/4 c. shredded mozzarella
cheese, divided
6-oz. can tomato paste
1/2 t. garlic powder
1/2 t. dried oregano
1/2 t. dried basil
1 c. milk
2 eggs, beaten
2/3 c. biscuit baking mix
1/4 t. pepper

Layer cottage cheese and Parmesan cheese in a greased 10" pie plate. Mix chicken, 1/2 cup mozzarella cheese, tomato paste and seasonings; spoon over Parmesan cheese. Beat remaining ingredients until smooth. Pour over chicken mixture. Bake at 400 degrees for 30 minutes. Top with remaining mozzarella cheese. Bake 5 to 8 minutes longer, or until a knife tip inserted in center comes out clean. Serves 6 to 8.

Kelly Alderson
Erie, PA

This crustless pie comes together easily when I use leftover chicken!

# Apricot-Glazed Carrots

6 c. carrots, peeled and sliced
3 T. butter, melted
1/3 c. apricot preserves
1/4 t. nutmeg
1/4 t. salt
2 t. lemon juice
Optional: 1 t. orange zest
Garnish: chopped fresh parsley

Place carrots in a large saucepan; cover with water. Bring to a boil and simmer until tender, 8 to 10 minutes; drain. In a bowl, combine remaining ingredients except parsley. Add carrots and stir to coat. Sprinkle with parsley. Serves 4 to 6.

47

Jill Burton
Gooseberry Patch

This is the only way my son Andy will eat cooked carrots!

# Sweet-and-Sauerkraut Brats

1-1/2 to 2 lbs. bratwurst, cut into
   bite-size pieces
27-oz. can sauerkraut
4 tart apples, cored, peeled
   and chopped
1/4 c. onion, chopped
1/4 c. brown sugar, packed
1 t. caraway seed
4 to 6 hard rolls, split
Garnish: spicy mustard

Place bratwurst into a slow cooker. Toss
together sauerkraut with juice, apples,
onion, brown sugar and caraway seed;
spoon over bratwurst. Cover and cook
on low setting for 4 to 5 hours, stirring
occasionally. Fill rolls, using a slotted
spoon. Serve with mustard on the side.
Makes 4 to 6 servings.

Jo Ann

I like to pop this into
the slow cooker before I
head out the door. When
I get home, I know a hearty
meal will be ready to
serve my family!

# Corn Sesame Sauté

10-oz. pkg. frozen corn
3 T. butter
1 clove garlic, minced
2 T. sesame seed
3 T. green pepper, chopped
3 T. red pepper, chopped
1/2 t. salt
1/4 t. fresh basil, chopped
1/8 t. pepper

Cook corn according to package instructions; drain and set aside. Heat remaining ingredients in a large saucepan for 5 minutes; add corn and heat through. Makes 6 servings.

49

**Ellen LaRose**
**Littleton, NH**

The perfect side for grilled chicken or steak. Or, serve with a loaf of bread and a side of applesauce for a meatless meal!

# Pound Cake S'mores

1 pound cake, sliced
1 to 2 c. mini marshmallows
12-oz. pkg. semi-sweet chocolate
   chips
12-oz. jar caramel ice cream
   topping
1/2 to 1 c. chopped walnuts

Place cake slices on an ungreased
baking sheet; sprinkle with
marshmallows and chocolate chips.
Place 4 to 6 inches under broiler;
broil for 2 to 3 minutes, or until
marshmallows are lightly golden.
Transfer 2 slices each to 6 to 8 serving
plates and drizzle with caramel topping;
sprinkle with walnuts. Makes 6 to
8 servings.

Cindy Schmitt
Oelwein, IA

This is the easiest and
quickest dessert. All the
flavors of s'mores without
having to build a campfire!

# Teresa's Potato Chip Fish

5-oz. pkg. kettle-cooked salt &
   vinegar potato chips
4 cod fillets
4 t. mayonnaise
Garnish: tartar sauce

Measure out half the chips and
set aside for another use. Place the
remaining chips in a plastic zipping
bag and crush. Line a baking sheet
with aluminum foil and spray with
non-stick vegetable spray. Arrange
fish on foil and pat dry. Spread
mayonnaise over top of each fillet;
cover each completely with crushed
chips. Bake at 400 degrees for
10 minutes, or until just cooked
through. Serve with tartar sauce.
Makes 4 servings.

51

**Tara Horton**
**Gooseberry Patch**

My sister Teresa and I
love salt & vinegar chips.
She made this for me
on my last visit!

# Scalloped Apples

10 tart apples, cored, peeled
  and sliced
1/3 c. sugar
2 T. cornstarch
1/2 to 1 t. cinnamon
1/8 t. nutmeg
2 T. butter, cubed

Place apples in a microwave-safe
2-1/2 quart bowl lightly sprayed with
non-stick vegetable spray; set aside.
Combine sugar, cornstarch and spices;
sprinkle over apples and toss to coat.
Dot with butter. Cover and microwave
on high setting for 15 minutes, or
until apples are tender, stirring every
5 minutes. Serves 6.

Jacqueline Kurtz
Reading, PA

A super-simple microwave
recipe that pairs nicely
with pork chop or
chicken dishes.

# Garlic Chicken Pizza

1/4 c. olive oil
1 lb. boneless, skinless chicken
   breasts, cubed
2 cloves garlic, pressed
1/2 t. fresh basil, chopped
1/2 t. fresh rosemary, chopped
2  12-inch Italian pizza crusts
14-oz. jar pizza sauce
16-oz. pkg. shredded mozzarella
   cheese
1 to 2 tomatoes, sliced
Garnish: grated Romano cheese

Heat olive oil in a large skillet over medium heat. Sauté chicken with garlic and herbs until chicken juices run clear; set aside. Arrange pizza crusts on 2 ungreased baking sheets; brush with olive oil from skillet. Spread with pizza sauce and chicken mixture; top with mozzarella cheese and tomato slices. Sprinkle with Romano cheese. Bake at 350 degrees until cheese bubbles and crusts are firm, about 5 minutes. Serves 8 to 10.

53

Becki Wunderlin
Louisville, KY
Garlic and olive oil taste so good...and make the kitchen smell wonderful!

# Double Crunch Bars

4 c. quick-cooking oats, uncooked
1 c. brown sugar, packed
3/4 c. butter, melted
1/2 c. honey
1/2 c. sweetened flaked coconut
1/2 c. semi-sweet chocolate chips
1/2 c. chopped nuts
1 t. vanilla extract
1 t. cinnamon
1 t. salt

Mix all ingredients together; press into a greased 15"x10" jelly-roll pan. Bake at 450 degrees for 10 to 12 minutes, or until golden; cool. Cut into bars. Makes about 2 dozen.

Jan Stafford
Chickamauga, GA

My friend, Debby, shared this recipe with me. Her 6 children and my 5 children all love these scrumptious bars!

# Autumn Apple Milkshake

14-oz. can sweetened
   condensed milk
1 c. applesauce
1/2 c. apple cider
1/2 t. apple pie spice
3 c. crushed ice
Garnish: cinnamon

In a blender, combine all ingredients
except ice and cinnamon. Gradually
add ice, blending until smooth.
Garnish with cinnamon. Serves
4 to 6.

55

### Vickie
This cool treat really
hits the spot after a long
session of raking leaves!

# Caramel Fudge Brownies

18-1/2 oz. pkg. German chocolate
  cake mix
3/4 c. butter, melted
5-oz. can evaporated milk, divided
14-oz. pkg. caramels, unwrapped
1 c. semi-sweet chocolate chips

Combine dry cake mix, butter and
1/3 cup evaporated milk. Spread half
of batter into a greased 13"x9" baking
pan (this layer will be very thin).
Bake at 350 degrees for 12 minutes.
Immediately after removing from oven,
sprinkle brownies with chocolate chips.
While crust is baking, melt caramels
and remaining evaporated milk in a
microwave-safe bowl for 3 minutes on
high setting. Stir caramel mixture and
pour over brownies. Spoon remaining
cake batter by heaping tablespoonfuls
over brownies; do not mix. Bake at
350 degrees for 15 to 17 minutes.
Makes 2 dozen.

Sue Roberson
Peoria, AZ

This recipe came from my
very special mother-in-law,
and although she's no longer
with us, her recipe continues
to be a family favorite.

# Taco Stacks

2 lbs. ground beef
1 onion, chopped
16-oz. can black beans, drained
   and rinsed
16-oz. can pinto beans, drained
   and rinsed
6  8-inch flour tortillas
26-oz. can tomato soup
1-1/2 c. shredded Cheddar
   cheese
Garnish: sour cream, salsa

Brown ground beef in a skillet;
drain. Stir in onion and beans.
Cook until onion is translucent.
Place a tortilla in bottom of a greased
13"x9" baking pan. Spoon 1/2 cup
soup over tortilla, layer with beef
mixture and sprinkle with 1/4 cup
cheese. Repeat, making 4 layers;
top with remaining tortilla, soup and
cheese. Cover with aluminum foil;
bake at 350 degrees for 30 minutes.
Serve with sour cream and salsa.
Serves 6.

57

Autumn Kozak
Lake City, MI

My daughter named this
recipe Taco Stacks when
she was 4...we've called
it that ever since!

# Jalapeño Cheese Log

16-oz. pkg. pasteurized process
   cheese spread
8-oz. pkg. cream cheese, softened
4-oz. can jalapeño peppers,
   drained and chopped
2-1/4 oz. can sliced black olives,
   drained

Place cheese spread between 2 pieces
of wax paper and roll out to 1/4-inch
thick rectangle; remove top piece of
wax paper and spread with cream
cheese. Sprinkle with peppers and
olives; roll up into a log while removing
the wax paper. Wrap in plastic wrap;
refrigerate until serving. Serves 8 to 10.

Pam Addison
Atkinson, NE

Bring out baskets of
crackers for this treat.

# Colossal Hero Sandwich

1 loaf Italian bread
2 c. romaine lettuce, shredded
2 T. Italian salad dressing
1/4 t. dried oregano
1/2 lb. sliced deli salami
6-oz. pkg. sliced provolone
    cheese
1 to 2 tomatoes, thinly sliced
1/2 lb. sliced deli ham
7-oz. jar roasted red peppers,
    drained and patted dry
6 pepperoncini, sliced
2-1/4 oz. can sliced black olives,
    drained
1 red onion, thinly sliced

Slice loaf in half lengthwise. With a fork, carefully hollow out the center of bottom loaf half and reserve for another use. Fill hollow with lettuce. Combine dressing and oregano in a small bowl; mix well and drizzle over lettuce. Layer remaining ingredients over lettuce. Cover with top of loaf and slice into individual portions. Serves 6 to 8.

Kathy Unruh
Fresno, CA

A classic! To make cutting easy, just push long toothpicks into the sandwich, then cut between the toothpicks with a serrated knife.

# Toasted Ravioli

9-oz. pkg. refrigerated
  cheese-filled ravioli
1/2 c. Italian-flavored seasoned
  dry bread crumbs
1/4 c. milk
1 egg
Garnish: grated Parmesan cheese,
  warm spaghetti sauce

Cook ravioli in boiling water for
3 minutes. Drain well and cool slightly.
Place bread crumbs in a shallow dish.
In another shallow dish, beat together
milk and egg. Dip ravioli in egg mixture
and let excess drip off. Dip in bread
crumbs to coat. Place ravioli on a
lightly greased baking sheet. Bake at
425 degrees for 15 minutes or until
crisp and golden. Sprinkle ravioli with
Parmesan cheese and serve with warm
spaghetti sauce. Makes 8 to 10 servings.

Diane Cohen
The Woodlands, TX
When we lived in Saint
Louis, these appetizers were
popular in restaurants. I
was excited to find a recipe
I could make at home.

# Cheddar-Bacon Balls

6 slices bacon, chopped
8-oz. pkg. Cheddar cheese,
    cubed
1/4 c. butter, cubed
2 T. fresh parsley, chopped
2 T. green onions, chopped
2 T. hot banana pepper rings
1/4 c. toasted pecans, finely
    chopped
assorted crackers

Cook bacon until crisp; drain, reserving one tablespoon drippings. In a blender or food processor, blend cheese, butter, parsley, green onions and pepper rings. Add bacon and reserved drippings; process until bacon is finely chopped. Chill mixture 3 hours, or until firm. Form mixture into one-inch balls. Roll balls in chopped pecans. Store in refrigerator up to 2 days before serving. Serve with crackers. Makes 2 dozen balls.

Linda Belon
Steubenville, OH
If the mixture softens during rolling, refrigerate it for 15 minutes.

# Greek Spread

1 c. plus 1 T. chopped almonds,
  divided
8-oz. pkg. crumbled feta cheese
7-oz. jar roasted red peppers,
  drained and chopped
1 clove garlic, chopped
2  8-oz. pkgs. cream cheese,
  softened
10-oz. pkg. frozen spinach,
  thawed and drained
crackers or toasted pita wedges

Line a 2-quart bowl with plastic wrap;
sprinkle in one tablespoon almonds.
In a separate bowl, mix together
1/2 cup almonds, feta cheese, peppers,
garlic, cream cheese and spinach; blend
well. Press into bowl over almonds.
Cover and chill overnight. Invert onto
a serving dish. Remove plastic wrap;
press remaining almonds onto the
outside. Serve with crackers or pita
wedges. Makes about 7 cups.

Stephanie Doyle
Lincoln University, PA
A must for our parties...
guests always request it!

# BBQ Turkey Sandwiches

2 T. butter
1/4 c. onion, chopped
8-oz. can tomato sauce
1 c. catsup
3 T. Worcestershire sauce
3 T. cider vinegar
1 T. brown sugar, packed
1/2 t. mustard
1/2 c. water
1/8 t. cinnamon
4 c. cooked turkey, cubed
8 hamburger buns, split

63

Melt butter in a saucepan over medium-high heat; sauté onion until softened. Add remaining ingredients except turkey and buns. Reduce heat to low; cover and simmer 30 minutes. In a large skillet over medium-low heat, combine turkey and enough of the sauce mixture to generously moisten. Cover and cook 10 minutes. Serve warm on hamburger buns. Makes 8 servings.

**Vickie**

We like to use the extra sauce as a dip for potato chips!

# Pumpkin Chowder

1/2-lb. bacon, diced
2 c. onion, chopped
2 t. curry powder
2 T. all-purpose flour
1-lb. pie pumpkin, peeled, seeded
   and chopped
2 potatoes, peeled and cubed
4 c. chicken broth
1 c. half-and-half
salt and pepper to taste
Garnish: toasted pumpkin seeds,
   sliced green onions

Brown bacon in a stockpot over medium heat for 5 minutes; add onion. Sauté for 10 minutes; add curry powder and flour, stirring until smooth and creamy, about 5 minutes. Add pumpkin, potatoes and broth; simmer until pumpkin and potatoes are tender, about 15 minutes. Pour in half-and-half; season with salt and pepper. Simmer for 5 minutes; do not boil. Spoon into soup bowls; garnish with pumpkin seeds and green onions. Serves 6.

Sandy Westendorp
Grand Rapids, MI
This blend of everyday ingredients is anything but ordinary.

# Fancy Caramel Apples

6  4-inch lollipop sticks
6 tart apples
14-oz. pkg. caramels, unwrapped
2 T. milk
6 tart apples
Garnish: colored candy
    sprinkles, sunflower seeds,
    mini chocolate chips

Insert lollipop sticks into tops of
apples. While making caramel
coating, place apples in freezer to
chill. Place caramels and milk in a
microwave-safe bowl; microwave on
high for 3 minutes, stirring once.
Allow to cool briefly. Remove apples
from freezer and dip into mixture.
Dip the bottoms into garnish of
choice. Place on a lightly buttered
baking sheet to cool. Chill in freezer
to set up if needed. Makes 6.

65

## Virginia Watson
## Scranton, PA

For a new twist, try
dipping the bottom half of
caramel-coated apples in
melted chocolate and then
rolling in chopped nuts.

# Game-Time Sausage Bites

**Marilyn Morel**
**Keene, NH**

These yummy bites are delicious for a holiday buffet or just sitting down together watching a special game. Be forewarned...they disappear quickly!

1 lb. Kielbasa sausage, cut into
    1/2-inch pieces
1 lb. hickory-smoked bacon, each
    slice cut into thirds

Wrap each sausage piece with a piece of bacon and secure with a wooden toothpick. Bake at 400 degrees on a lightly greased broiler pan for 15 minutes; turn and bake an additional 15 to 20 minutes, until bacon is golden and crisp. Drain on paper towels. Serve with Marmalade Dipping Sauce. Makes 30 appetizers.

**Marmalade Dipping Sauce:**

1/2 c. orange marmalade
1 T. lime juice
1 T. soy sauce
2 T. Dijon mustard
hot pepper sauce to taste

Combine all ingredients in a microwave-safe bowl. Microwave on high for one minute.

# Maple-Topped Sweet Potato Skins

6 sweet potatoes
1/2 c. cream cheese, softened
1/4 c. sour cream
2 t. cinnamon, divided
2 t. nutmeg, divided
2 t. ground ginger, divided
2 c. chopped walnuts or pecans
3 T. butter, softened
1/4 c. brown sugar, packed
Garnish: warm maple syrup,
    additional nuts

67

Pierce potatoes with a fork. Bake
at 400 degrees or microwave on
high setting until tender; cool. Slice
each potato in half lengthwise; scoop
out baked insides, keeping skins
intact. Place potato skins on an
ungreased baking sheet. Mash baked
potato in a bowl until smooth; add
cream cheese, sour cream and one
teaspoon each of spices. Mix well and
spoon into potato skins. In a bowl,
mix nuts, butter, brown sugar and
remaining spices; sprinkle over top.
Bake at 400 degrees for 15 minutes.
Drizzle with warm maple syrup;
garnish as desired. Makes one dozen.

Linda Corcoran
Metuchen, NJ
I love finding these
appetizers on a buffet
table...they're
absolutely wonderful!

# Touchdown Butterscotch Dip

2  11-oz. pkgs. butterscotch chips
5-oz. can evaporated milk
2/3 c. chopped pecans
1 T. rum extract
apple and pear wedges

Combine butterscotch chips and
evaporated milk in a slow cooker.
Cover and cook on low setting for
45 to 50 minutes, or until chips are
softened; stir until smooth. Stir in
pecans and extract. Serve warm with
fruit. Makes about 3 cups.

Melanie Lowe
Dover, DE

Mom likes to make
this creamy dip when the
"big game" is on!

# Tex-Mex Mini Chicken Cups

1-1/2 lbs. boneless, skinless
  chicken breasts, cooked and
  shredded
1 c. ranch salad dressing or
  sour cream
1/4 t. salt
1/4 t. pepper
8-oz. pkg. shredded Monterey
  Jack cheese
2 T. chili powder
48 wonton wrappers
1 c. red or green pepper, finely
  chopped
Garnish: salsa, sour cream,
  guacamole

Combine chicken, salad dressing
or sour cream, salt and pepper. In
a separate bowl, combine cheese
with chili powder; set aside. Press
2 wonton wrappers each into
24 lightly greased muffin cups. Bake
at 350 degrees for 5 minutes, or until
lightly golden; remove from oven and
cool. Spoon one tablespoon chicken
filling into each wonton cup; sprinkle
with cheese mixture and top with
chopped pepper. Return to oven;
bake for an additional 10 minutes,
or until cheese is melted. Serve with
salsa, sour cream and guacamole.
Makes 2 dozen.

Trisha Fipps
Dunbar, WI
I usually mix up the
ingredients for the filling
ahead of time, then put
them together right before
company arrives.

# Grandma Paris' Bambinis

1 c. ricotta cheese
1/2 c. shredded mozzarella cheese
1/4 c. grated Parmesan cheese
10-oz. tube refrigerated large
   flaky biscuits
20 thin slices pepperoni

Combine cheeses in a bowl; set aside.
Halve each biscuit horizontally and
gently shape each half into a 4"x2-1/2"
oval. Place one pepperoni slice and
one tablespoon cheese mixture in the
upper half of each oval; fold dough
up and over filling, pinching closed.
Repeat with remaining ingredients.
Arrange on a lightly greased baking
sheet; bake at 350 degrees for
20 minutes. Makes 20.

Kristin
Santangelo-Winterhoff
Jersey City, NJ

My grandma and mom entered
this recipe in the
Rochester, NY Cook-Off
and won first prize!

# Cranberry Tea

6 c. water, divided
2 family-size or 8 regular teabags
1 t. whole cloves
2  2-1/2 inch cinnamon sticks
2 c. sugar
2 c. cranberry juice cocktail
1 c. orange juice
1/4 c. lemon juice

In a large pot, bring 4 cups water to a boil. Add teabags, cloves and cinnamon sticks; cover and steep for 5 minutes. Strain, discarding teabags and spices. Stir in remaining water and other ingredients. Stir until sugar is dissolved. Serve warm or over ice. Makes 4 quarts.

71

Nola Coons
Gooseberry Patch

A special treat for tea lovers. So yummy with cranberry scones!

# Zucchini Patties

1-1/2 c. zucchini, shredded and
   pressed dry
1 c. panko bread crumbs
2 T. onion, finely chopped
2 T. all-purpose flour
1 T. mayonnaise
1 t. seafood seasoning
2 eggs, beaten
oil for frying
Garnish: applesauce, sour cream
   or catsup

In a large bowl, combine zucchini,
bread crumbs, onion, flour,
mayonnaise and seasoning. Add eggs,
stirring well to combine. Shape into
10 patties. Add enough oil in a large
skillet to equal 1/2-inch depth; heat
over medium heat until hot. Fry patties
for one to 2 minutes per side, until
golden. Drain on paper towels. Serve
with sour cream, applesauce or catsup.
Makes 10 servings.

Linda McGowan
Riverside, RI

My mom made these for
snacks and appetizers. A
great way to use up your
zucchini harvest!

# Swampwater Dressing

1 c. oil
6 T. cider vinegar
1/2 c. sugar
1 t. celery seed
1/2 t. salt
1/4 t. pepper

Combine ingredients in a jar or plastic container with a tight-fitting lid; cover. Shake well until dressing is blended and sugar dissolves. Keep refrigerated. Makes about 1-1/2 cups.

73

**Jennie Gist**
**Gooseberry Patch**
Serve this zingy dressing alongside a leafy green salad at your Halloween "Boo"-ffet!

# Honey-Lime Wings

1/4 c. honey
juice and zest of one lime
1 clove garlic, minced
1/4 t. salt
1/4 t. pepper
1/2 c. all-purpose flour
3 lbs. chicken wings
oil for deep frying

Mix together honey, lime juice and zest, garlic, salt and pepper in a large bowl; set aside. Place flour in a large plastic zipping bag and add wings, shaking to coat. Heat one inch of oil in a large skillet over medium-high heat. Add wings in batches; cook until golden and juices run clear. Drain; place wings in honey mixture and toss to coat well. Serve hot. Makes about 3 dozen.

Jen Stout
Blandon, PA

Crisp party wings with a refreshing sweet-tart seasoning. For Halloween, you can call them bat wings!

# Hauntingly-Good Candy Cake

12 favorite fun-size candy bars
2 T. milk
18-1/2 oz. pkg. white cake mix
3 eggs, beaten
1 c. water
1/3 c. oil
2 T. all-purpose flour
1/8 t. salt
16-oz. container chocolate
  frosting
Garnish: chopped candy bars,
  candy corn

Combine candy bars and milk in a
heavy saucepan over medium heat;
stir until candy melts. Remove from
heat; set aside to cool for 5 minutes.
Beat dry cake mix, eggs, water and
oil together with an electric mixer
on low speed for 30 seconds; increase
speed to high, beating 2 minutes.
Add 2/3 cup batter, flour and salt
into candy bar mixture; stir well
and set aside. Pour remaining
batter into a buttered and floured
13"x9" baking pan; drop candy batter
by tablespoonfuls into cake batter.
Swirl batters together with a knife.
Bake at 350 degrees for 30 to
35 minutes. Cool completely; frost.
Sprinkle with garnishes. Makes
20 to 24 servings.

JoAnn

A terrific use for
all those bags of
Halloween candy!

# Silver Moons

1 T. sugar
1/4 t. cinnamon
16.3-oz. tube refrigerated large
    biscuits
1 c. apple pie filling
4 t. butter, melted
Garnish: powdered sugar

In a small bowl, combine sugar and cinnamon; set aside. Separate dough into 8 biscuits. Press each biscuit into a 5-inch circle. Arrange biscuits on greased baking sheets. Place 2 tablespoons pie filling on each circle half. Fold biscuits over filling; seal edges with a fork. Pierce each pie a few times with fork. Brush pies with melted butter and sprinkle with sugar mixture. Bake at 375 degrees for 15 to 20 minutes. Sprinkle with powdered sugar. Serve warm. Makes 8.

Dale Duncan
Waterloo, IA
Your little werewolves
will be howling for more!

# Spicy Citrus Cider

8 c. apple juice
2-1/4 c. water
1-1/2 c. orange juice
1/4 c. molasses
3  4-inch cinnamon sticks
1 T. whole cloves
Garnish: apple and orange slices

Combine all ingredients except
fruit slices in a large saucepan
over medium heat. Simmer for
10 minutes, stirring occasionally.
Strain before serving. Garnish
with fruit slices. Makes about
3 quarts.

77

Ellen Folkman
Crystal Beach, FL

Keep this flavorful
beverage warm in a slow
cooker...everyone can
help themselves.

# Centipede Cakes

18-1/4 oz. pkg. yellow cake mix
16-oz. container vanilla frosting
few drops red and yellow food
    coloring
3 c. orange, purple, black and
    green candy-coated chocolates
12 strands red licorice laces, cut
    into 2-inch pieces

Prepare cake mix according to package directions, baking in 24 paper-lined muffin cups. Let cool completely. Tint frosting with food coloring to make 1/2 cup orange and 1-1/2 cups yellow frosting; frost cupcakes. Set 2 cupcakes aside. Decorate reserved cupcakes using black chocolates to make eyes and mouths. Decorate remaining cupcakes with chocolates as desired. Arrange cupcakes in S-shapes on 2 serving platters. To create the legs, press licorice laces on opposite sides of each yellow cupcake. Makes 2 dozen.

Tina Dillon
Parma, OH

I have my grandchildren over around Halloween for hot chocolate and cupcake decorating! In the summer it's lemonade and caterpillars!

# Pumpkin Patch Cheese Ball

16-oz. pkg. shredded extra-sharp
    Cheddar cheese
8-oz. pkg. cream cheese,
    softened
8-oz. container chive & onion
    cream cheese
2 t. paprika
1/2 t. cayenne pepper
honey-wheat twist pretzel
flat-leaf parsley leaves
assorted crackers

In a medium bowl, combine cheeses
and spices. Cover and refrigerate
for 4 hours. Shape mixture into a
ball; lightly press into a pumpkin
shape. Smooth surface with a table
knife. Press pretzel and parsley
into top of cheese ball for pumpkin
stem and leaf. Serve with crackers.
Makes 10 to 12 servings.

**Vickie**
Makes a tasty cheese
ball any time of year...
but especially fun
at Halloween!

# Cream-Filled Witches' Hats

1-3/4 c. whipping cream, divided
6-oz. pkg. milk chocolate chips
4  1-oz. sqs. semi-sweet baking
  chocolate, chopped
1/2 t. shortening
12 chocolate-coated ice cream
  cones
12 thin chocolate wafer cookies
Garnish: candy sprinkles

Bring 1/2 cup cream to a boil in a
saucepan; remove from heat. Stir in
chips until melted and smooth; spoon
into a bowl. Let cool, stirring
occasionally. Beat remaining cream
with an electric mixer on high speed
until stiff peaks form; fold into
chocolate mixture. Chill. In a
microwave-safe bowl, melt baking
chocolate and shortening on high
for one to 2 minutes; stir. Dip tips
of cones into chocolate, then into
sprinkles. Chill until set. To serve,
spoon cream into cones; set each on
a cookie. Makes 12.

Kerry Mayer
Dunham Springs, LA

Short on time? Fill the
hats with creamy chocolate
whipped topping instead.

# Spiderweb Cookies

16-1/2 oz. tube refrigerated sugar
 cookie dough
3 c. powdered sugar
3 T. light corn syrup
1/2 t. vanilla extract
3 T. plus 3 t. milk, divided
2 T. baking cocoa

Slice dough into 16 rounds. Place
2 inches apart on ungreased baking
sheets. Bake at 350 degrees for
12 to 14 minutes. Transfer to a wire
rack to cool. Blend powdered sugar,
corn syrup, vanilla and 3 tablespoons
plus one teaspoon milk until smooth.
Measure 1/3 cup of frosting mixture
into a small bowl; stir in cocoa and
remaining milk. Transfer chocolate
frosting to a plastic zipping bag; snip
off corner. Turn cookies so flat sides
are up. Working on one cookie at a
time, spread white frosting over top.
Beginning in the center, pipe on a
spiral of chocolate frosting. Starting
in center of spiral, pull a knife tip
through the spiral to create spiderweb
pattern. Makes 16.

81

Athena Colegrove
Big Springs, TX
Tuck these in cellophane
bags, tie with twine and
attach a spider ring...
creepy and cute!

# Herb Garden Turkey Breast

8-1/2 lb. turkey breast
3 T. lemon juice, divided
2 T. oil, divided
2 cloves garlic, minced
1 t. lemon zest
1 t. dried thyme
1/2 t. dried sage
1-1/4 t. salt
3/4 t. pepper
prepared stuffing

Place turkey breast on a rack in an ungreased shallow roasting pan; loosen skin on top without removing it. Combine one tablespoon lemon juice, one tablespoon oil, garlic, lemon zest and seasonings; spread under loosened skin. Combine remaining lemon juice and oil; set aside. Bake, uncovered, at 350 degrees for 2-1/2 to 3 hours, basting every 15 to 20 minutes with lemon mixture. Turkey is done when a meat thermometer inserted into thickest part reads 180 degrees. Remove to a serving platter; let stand for 10 minutes before slicing. Serve with your favorite prepared stuffing (recipe for pictured stuffing is on page 93). Makes 14 to 16 servings.

Wendy Jacobs
Idaho Falls, ID

Even more delicious made with fresh thyme and sage...just double the amounts called for.

# Acorn Squash Fruit Cups

2 acorn squash, halved and
  seeds removed
1/4 t. salt
2 c. tart apples, cored and
  chopped
3/4 c. cranberries
1/4 c. sugar
1/4 c. brown sugar, packed
2 T. butter, melted
1/4 t. cinnamon
1/8 t. nutmeg

Place squash cut-side down in an
ungreased 13"x9" baking pan. Add
one inch of hot water to the pan.
Bake, uncovered, at 350 degrees
for 30 minutes. Drain water from
pan; turn squash over so cut side
is up. Sprinkle with salt. Combine
remaining ingredients and spoon
into squash. Bake, uncovered, for
40 to 50 minutes longer, or until
squash is tender. Makes 4 servings.

Janis Parr
Ontario, Canada

The rich flavors of apple,
cranberry and succulent
acorn squash combine to make
this dish so delicious!
It's like a dessert that's
good for you!

# Harvest Apple Cheesecake

2 c. graham cracker crumbs
1/3 c. brown sugar, packed
1/2 c. butter, melted and divided
1 T. cinnamon
3 apples, cored, peeled and sliced
  into 12 rings
4 eggs, beaten
3/4 c. sugar
8-oz. container ricotta cheese
8-oz. pkg. cream cheese, softened
2 t. vanilla extract
8-oz. container whipping cream
Garnish: cinnamon

Combine cracker crumbs, brown sugar, 1/4 cup butter and cinnamon. Press onto bottom and partway up sides of an ungreased 9" springform pan. In a skillet, sauté apple slices on both sides in remaining butter. Arrange 6 apple slices on prepared crust. In a bowl, beat eggs, sugar, ricotta cheese, cream cheese and vanilla until smooth. Add whipping cream and blend well. Pour cheese mixture into pan. Arrange remaining apple slices on top and press apples slightly under the mixture. Sprinkle top with cinnamon. Bake at 450 degrees for 10 minutes, then reduce heat to 300 degrees and bake for 50 to 55 minutes. Cool and refrigerate overnight. Serves 8 to 12.

Brenda Smith
Gooseberry Patch

After we come home from apple picking, my family helps me make this delicious dessert!

# Ham & Potato Chowder

1/4 c. butter
1 onion, chopped
3 cloves garlic, minced
1/4 c. green pepper, chopped
1/4 c. red pepper, chopped
2 carrots, peeled and diced
4  14-1/2 oz. cans chicken broth
4 c. redskin potatoes, quartered
1/4 t. nutmeg
1-1/2 t. dried thyme
2 T. all-purpose flour
2/3 c. water
2 c. milk
11-oz. can corn, drained
2 c. cooked ham, diced
oyster crackers

Melt butter in a large pot over medium heat; sauté onion, garlic, peppers and carrots until tender. Add broth, potatoes, nutmeg and thyme. Reduce heat; cover and simmer for 1-1/2 hours. Bring to a boil. Whisk flour and water together and slowly add to chowder. Boil until thickened. Remove from heat and slowly pour in milk; stir in corn and ham. Serve with oyster crackers. Serves 6.

Amy Butcher
Columbus, GA
Crusty bread from the bakery makes this a comforting meal!

# Fresh Cranberry Relish

12-oz. pkg. cranberries
2 apples, cored, peeled and
    quartered
2 pears, cored, peeled and
    quartered
2 oranges, peeled and sectioned
orange zest to taste
honey to taste
Optional: 1/2 c. coarsely chopped
    pecans

Coarsely chop cranberries, apples,
pears and oranges in a food processor.
Mix in orange zest, honey and nuts,
if using. Chill until serving time.
Makes about 8 cups.

Karen Healey
Rutland, MA

I make this simple recipe
every Thanksgiving and
Christmas. I garnish it
with stars cut from the
orange peel with a small
cookie cutter.

# Cran-Orange Pork Medallions

1 to 1-1/2 lb. pork tenderloin,
   cut into 1-inch slices
1/2 t. garlic powder
1/2 t. coriander
1/2 t. salt
1/4 t. pepper
2 T. olive oil
1 red onion, chopped
1/2 c. orange marmalade
1/4 c. orange juice
1/4 c. sweetened dried
   cranberries
2 T. balsamic vinegar

87

Place pork slices between 2 pieces of wax paper. Using a rolling pin, flatten to 1/4-inch thickness. Combine seasonings; sprinkle over both sides of pork. In a large skillet, sauté pork in oil for 3 minutes on each side, or until juices run clear. Remove and keep warm. In same skillet, sauté onion in pan juices for 5 minutes, or until tender. Stir in remaining ingredients; bring to a boil. Reduce heat; return pork to skillet. Simmer, uncovered, for 5 minutes, or until sauce is thickened. Makes 4 servings.

**JoAnn**
Ready in just 30 minutes...
what a time-saver!

# Homemade Turkey Pot Pie

1/3 c. margarine
1/3 c. onion, chopped
1/3 c. all-purpose flour
1/2 t. salt
1/4 t. pepper
1-3/4 c. turkey broth
2/3 c. milk
2-1/2 to 3 c. cooked turkey, chopped
10-oz. pkg. frozen peas and carrots, thawed
2  9-inch pie crusts

Melt margarine in a large saucepan over low heat. Stir in onion, flour, salt and pepper. Cook, stirring constantly, until mixture is bubbly; remove from heat. Stir in broth and milk. Heat to boiling, stirring constantly. Boil and stir for one minute. Mix in turkey, peas and carrots; set aside. Roll out each pie crust into an 11-inch by 11-inch square. Place one into a 9"x9" baking pan. Spoon turkey mixture into pan. Place remaining crust over filling; turn edges under and crimp. Bake at 425 degrees for about 35 minutes, or until crust is golden. Makes 9 servings.

Sarah Sullivan
Andrews, NC

Mmm...everybody's favorite after-Thanksgiving comfort food!

# Lucy's Pumpkin-Chocolate Chip Cake

15-oz. can pumpkin
4 eggs, beaten
1 c. oil
2 c. sugar
3 c. all-purpose flour
2 t. baking powder
2 t. baking soda
2 t. cinnamon
12-oz. pkg. semi-sweet chocolate
   chips, divided

In a large bowl, mix together pumpkin, eggs, oil and sugar. Mix in flour, baking powder, baking soda and cinnamon. Stir in half the chocolate chips. Pour batter into a greased and floured Bundt® pan. Sprinkle remaining chocolate chips over batter. Bake at 350 degrees for one hour, or until golden and a toothpick tests clean. Cool and remove from pan. Makes 12 to 16 servings.

Suzanne Morelli
Foster, RI

This is a family favorite passed down by my mother-in-law, Lucy Morelli.

# Amish Pear Pie

1/3 c. sugar
1 T. cornstarch
1/8 t. salt
5 c. pears, cored, peeled
  and sliced
9-inch pie crust
Optional: vanilla ice cream

Mix sugar, cornstarch and salt together; add pear slices and toss to coat. Spread in pie crust; sprinkle with Cheese Topping. Bake on lower oven rack at 425 degrees for 25 to 30 minutes, or until pears are tender. Serve with a scoop of ice cream, if desired. Makes 8 servings.

**Cheese Topping:**
1/2 c. all-purpose flour
1/4 t. salt
1/2 c. sugar
1/2 c. shredded sharp Cheddar
  cheese
1/4 c. butter, melted

Combine ingredients together until mixture resembles coarse crumbs.

Rosie Bertolini
Santa Rosa, CA

Try this...you'll be surprised and delighted by the combination!

# Finnish Sweet Potato Soup

3 sweet potatoes, peeled and
    sliced
2 c. chicken broth
1-1/2 c. light cream or
    half-and-half
1 t. sugar
1/8 t. ground cloves
1/8 t. nutmeg
salt to taste
Optional: sour cream, nutmeg

Put sweet potatoes and broth in a
slow cooker. Cover and cook on
high setting for 2 to 3 hours, until
potatoes are tender. Purée in a
blender or food processor. Return
puréed potatoes to slow cooker; add
remaining ingredients. Cover and
cook on high setting for an additional
one to 2 hours. Serve hot or chilled
with a dollop of sour cream and a
sprinkle of nutmeg, if desired.
Makes about 4 servings.

**Sherry Saarinen
Hancock, MI**

Sweet potatoes grow
abundantly here in the Upper
Peninsula of Michigan. I've
found a lot of uses for
them, but none is as tasty
as this soup!

# Country Harvest
# Maple Pot Roast

2-lb. boneless beef chuck roast
1/2 c. orange juice
1/2 c. maple syrup
2 T. red wine vinegar
1 T. Worcestershire sauce
2 t. orange zest
1/4 t. salt
1/4 t. pepper
2 carrots, peeled and cut into
   2-inch pieces
2 stalks celery, cut into
   2-inch pieces
1 onion, chopped
2 potatoes, peeled and cut into
   2-inch cubes

Brown roast over medium heat in a Dutch oven sprayed with non-stick vegetable spray. In a bowl, combine orange juice, syrup, vinegar, Worcestershire sauce, orange zest, salt and pepper. Pour over roast. Bring to a boil. Reduce heat; cover and simmer one hour. Add carrots, celery and onions; cover and simmer 20 minutes. Add potatoes; cover and simmer for 20 minutes, until tender. Makes 4 to 6 servings.

**Lisa Windhorn**
**Seattle, WA**

Just as tasty made in the slow cooker. Cook on low setting for 8 to 10 hours, or on high setting for 4 to 6 hours.

# Chestnut Stuffing

1 lb. whole chestnuts
2 qts. water
1 onion, chopped
1 T. butter
2 apples, cored and chopped
3/4 c. soft bread, cubed
1 T. fresh parsley
1/2 t. dried thyme
1/4 t. pepper
1/4 c. chicken broth

93

Cut an X in the flat side of each
chestnut using a knife point.
Boil chestnuts in water for 15 to
25 minutes. Drain and cool. Peel
chestnuts and cut into quarters.
Set aside. In a skillet, combine onion
and butter; sauté until tender. Add
chestnuts and remaining ingredients,
mixing well. Spoon into a greased
1-1/2 quart casserole dish. Bake,
covered, at 350 degrees for
30 minutes. Uncover and bake
an additional 15 to 25 minutes.
Serves 6 to 8.

## Vickie

Serve your Thanksgiving
turkey with a traditional
recipe from New England.

# Loaded Mashed Potato Casserole

5 to 6 potatoes, peeled and cubed
1/2 c. milk
8-oz. pkg. cream cheese, softened
8-oz. container sour cream
2 t. dried parsley
1 t. garlic salt
1/4 t. nutmeg
3/4 c. shredded Cheddar cheese
12 slices bacon, crisply cooked
    and crumbled

Cover potatoes with water in a large saucepan; bring to boil over medium heat. Reduce heat; simmer for 20 to 25 minutes. Drain well. Mash until light and fluffy. In a large bowl, beat together all ingredients except Cheddar cheese and bacon until smooth and creamy. Spoon into a lightly greased 13"x9" baking pan; sprinkle with cheese and bacon. Cover and bake at 350 degrees for 30 minutes, or until heated through. Serves 10 to 12.

Nancy Girard
Chesapeake, VA

This homestyle casserole is filled with so many good things.

# Ben's Pecan Blondies

1 c. sugar
1/2 c. brown sugar, packed
1/2 c. butter, softened
2 eggs, beaten
1 t. vanilla extract
1-1/2 c. all-purpose flour
1 t. baking powder
1/2 t. salt
1/2 c. chopped pecans
Garnish: pecan halves

Beat sugar, brown sugar and butter until fluffy. Blend in eggs and vanilla. Mix in flour, baking powder and salt. Stir in chopped pecans. Pour batter into a greased 13"x9" baking pan. Bake at 350 degrees for 25 to 35 minutes. Cool one hour; frost with Browned Butter Frosting. Cut into bars and garnish with pecan halves. Makes 3 dozen.

**Browned Butter Frosting:**

2 T. butter
2 c. powdered sugar
1/4 t. vanilla extract
2 to 4 T. milk

Heat butter in saucepan over medium heat until light golden brown. Remove from heat. Stir in powdered sugar, vanilla and enough milk for desired consistency.

Diana Chaney
Olathe, KS

My nephew, Ben, has been requesting these since he was 9...he's now 34!

# Harvest Home Roast Turkey

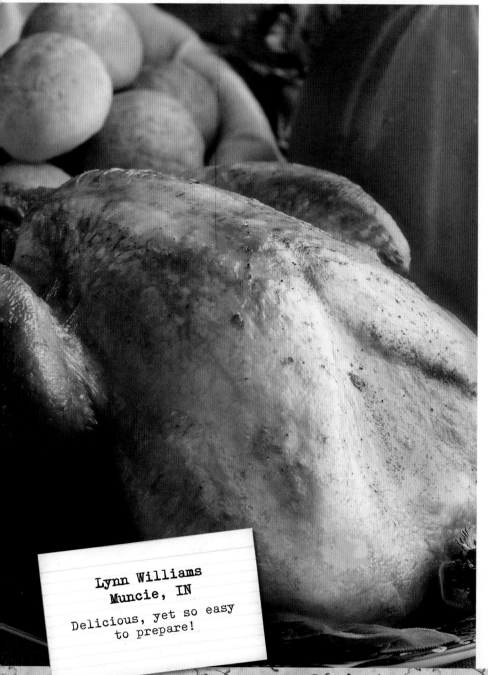

14 to 15-lb. turkey, thawed
2 cloves garlic, halved and divided
1 t. seasoning salt, divided
1 onion, quartered
1 bunch fresh parsley
2 fresh thyme sprigs
5 to 6 leaves fresh sage
2 T. olive oil
pepper to taste

Pat turkey dry. Remove giblets and neck; reserve for another use. Rub inside of turkey with one clove garlic and 1/2 teaspoon salt; stuff with remaining garlic, onion and herbs. Place turkey breast-side up on a rack in a large roaster pan. Brush oil over turkey; sprinkle with remaining seasoning salt and pepper to taste. Roast turkey, uncovered, at 325 degrees about 3 to 3-1/2 hours, basting occasionally with pan drippings, until a meat thermometer inserted into thickest part of thigh registers 180 degrees. If needed, tent turkey with aluminum foil to prevent browning too quickly. Let turkey stand 15 to 20 minutes before carving; discard garlic, onion and herbs. Serves 10 to 12.

Lynn Williams
Muncie, IN
Delicious, yet so easy to prepare!

# Green Bean Bundles

1/2 lb. bacon, sliced crosswise
4  14-1/2 oz. cans whole green
   beans, drained
1 c. brown sugar, packed and
   divided
3/4 c. margarine, divided

Microwave bacon on a microwave-safe plate until partially cooked, about one minute. Drain bacon on paper towels. Gather 8 to 10 green beans in a bundle and wrap with a strip of bacon. Place bundle seam-side down in a greased 13"x9" baking pan. Repeat with remaining ingredients. Top each bundle with one tablespoon brown sugar and one tablespoon margarine. Bake, uncovered, at 350 degrees for 30 minutes, or until bacon is done. Makes 12 servings.

97

Janet Stewart
Owensboro, KY
This is a fancy way to serve green beans. With bacon and brown sugar, it is also very yummy.

# Orange-Cranberry Cake

18-1/2 oz. pkg. white cake mix
3.4-oz. pkg. instant vanilla
    pudding mix
1 t. orange zest
1/2 c. butter, melted and cooled
4 eggs, beaten
1 c. milk
1-1/2 c. cranberries, chopped
1 c. dried apricots, coarsely
    chopped

Combine dry cake mix, dry pudding mix and orange zest. Add melted butter, eggs and milk; beat according to cake package directions. Fold in cranberries and apricots. Spoon batter into a lightly greased tube pan. Bake at 350 degrees for 55 to 65 minutes, or until a toothpick tests clean. Cool in pan for 20 minutes. Remove from pan and cool completely. Drizzle with Orange Glaze. Makes 12 to 16 servings.

**Orange Glaze:**

1 c. vanilla frosting
1 T. frozen orange juice
    concentrate, thawed

Stir ingredients together in a microwave-safe bowl. Microwave on medium power for 30 to 45 seconds, or until glaze is desired consistency.

Tiffany Brinkley
Broomfield, CO

My book club friends ask me to make this when it's my turn to host!

# Tangy Corn Casserole

10-oz. pkg. frozen corn, thawed
  and drained
1/2 c. onion, chopped
1/2 c. green pepper, sliced
  into strips
1/2 c. water
1 c. yellow squash, chopped
1 tomato, chopped
1 c. shredded Cheddar cheese,
  divided
2/3 c. cornmeal
1/2 c. milk
2 eggs, beaten
3/4 t. salt
1/4 t. pepper
1/4 t. hot pepper sauce

In a saucepan, combine corn, onion,
green pepper and water; bring to a
boil. Reduce heat to medium-low;
cover and simmer 5 minutes. Do not
drain. In a bowl, combine squash,
tomato, 3/4 cup cheese and
remaining ingredients. Stir corn
mixture into squash mixture.
Transfer to a greased 1-1/2 quart
casserole dish. Bake, uncovered, at
350 degrees for 45 to 50 minutes.
Garnish with remaining cheese.
Serves 6 to 8.

Dave Slyh
Galloway, OH

A great side dish for
celebrations or even
for brunch.

# Cheesy Garlic Rolls

1/2 c. butter, cubed
2 t. garlic powder
2  12-ct. pkgs. frozen dinner roll
   dough
1/2 c. grated Parmesan cheese,
   divided

Microwave butter in a microwave-safe bowl until melted; mix in garlic powder. Place frozen rolls in a greased 13"x9" baking pan. Brush butter mixture over rolls; sprinkle with 1/4 cup Parmesan cheese. Let rolls rise according to package instructions. Bake at 350 degrees for 15 to 20 minutes, until golden. Brush with remaining butter mixture and sprinkle with remaining Parmesan cheese. Makes 2 dozen rolls.

Robin Struble
Bluff City, KS

I came up with this easy-to-prepare recipe while working at our school's kitchen. Great with lasagna or soup!

# Mom's Caramel Sweet Potatoes

6 sweet potatoes, peeled and
    cubed
1/2 c. brown sugar, packed
1 c. butter, sliced and divided
1 t. vanilla extract
1/2 t. imitation butter flavoring
1 c. sugar
1 c. half-and-half

In a large saucepan, cover sweet potatoes with water. Bring to a boil over medium-high heat. Cook until fork-tender; drain. With an electric mixer on medium speed, beat until smooth. Add brown sugar, 1/2 cup butter, vanilla and butter flavoring to sweet potatoes; mix well. Pour into a buttered large serving bowl; make a well in center for sauce. Keep warm until caramel sauce is added. To make the caramel sauce, combine sugar, half-and-half and remaining butter in a large skillet. Cook over medium-low heat for 20 to 25 minutes, until honey-colored and slightly thickened. Pour sauce into well in sweet potatoes. Serves 8 to 10.

101

Jennifer Mathis
Tupelo, MS
These are the best sweet potatoes you'll ever have! Sweet and creamy...a must-have on the holiday table. My family has enjoyed this for years.

# Harvest Fruit & Nut Pie

4 Granny Smith apples, cored,
  peeled and sliced
1 c. cranberries
1/2 c. pineapple chunks
1/2 c. chopped walnuts
1 c. sugar
2/3 c. brown sugar, packed
1/4 c. all-purpose flour
1 t. cinnamon
1/4 t. nutmeg
4  9-inch deep-dish pie crusts
3 T. butter

Mix together apples, cranberries,
pineapple, walnuts and sugar. Sift
together brown sugar, flour, cinnamon
and nutmeg; add to apple mixture.
Arrange 2 pie crusts in two 9" pie
plates. Divide mixture equally between
pie crusts; dot each with butter and
cover with top pie crust, crimping to
seal. Bake at 400 degrees for 45
minutes. Makes 2 pies.

Angie Venable
Gooseberry Patch

Our family loves this!
I make one to share and
one to enjoy at home.

# Country Harvest
# Honey-Pecan Chicken

1/2 c. all-purpose flour
1 t. salt
1/3 t. pepper
1 lb. boneless, skinless chicken
  breasts
3 T. butter
1/3 c. honey
1/4 c. chopped pecans

In a shallow dish, combine flour, salt
and pepper. Place chicken breasts
between 2 pieces of wax paper.
Using a rolling pin, flatten to
1/4-inch thickness. Coat chicken
in flour mixture. In a large skillet,
melt butter over medium-high heat.
Add chicken and brown on both
sides. Transfer to a warm plate.
Stir honey and pecans into pan
drippings. Heat through, stirring
constantly. Pour sauce over chicken.
Serves 4.

Amy Bell
Arlington, TN

This flavorful dish is
fancy enough for guests,
yet simple enough for
a weeknight!

# Homestyle Beef Pot Pie

16-oz. pkg. frozen mixed
    vegetables
2 T. water
1/2 t. dried thyme
12-oz. jar mushroom gravy
1 lb. roast beef, cubed
pepper to taste
8-oz. tube refrigerated
    crescent rolls

Combine vegetables, water and thyme
in a skillet. Cook over medium heat
until vegetables are thawed, about
3 minutes. Stir in gravy; bring to a
boil. Remove from heat. Add beef;
mix well. Transfer to a 9" glass pie
plate and sprinkle with pepper.
Separate crescent rolls into 8 triangles.
Starting at wide ends, roll up halfway;
arrange over beef mixture so pointed
ends are directed to the center. Bake at
375 degrees for 17 to 19 minutes, or
until rolls are golden. Serves 6 to 8.

Doris Stegner
Gooseberry Patch

This traditional dish
is a hearty meal
all by itself.

# Honey-Pumpkin Pie

15-oz. can pumpkin
3/4 c. honey
1/2 t. salt
1 t. cinnamon
1/2 t. ground ginger
1/4 t. ground cloves
1/4 t. nutmeg
3 eggs, beaten
2/3 c. evaporated milk
1/2 c. milk
9-inch pie crust

Stir together pumpkin, honey, salt and spices in a large bowl. Add eggs and mix well; stir in both milks. Place pie crust in a 9" pie plate; flute edges, forming a high rim to hold pumpkin filling. Do not pierce crust. Place pie plate on oven rack; pour in filling. Bake at 375 degrees for 55 to 60 minutes, or until set. Let cool before serving. Makes 6 to 8 servings.

**Sharon Demers**
**Dolores, CO**

Whenever I can, I make this pie with farm-fresh eggs and honey from a local beekeeper.

# Over-Stuffed Shells

10-oz. pkg. frozen chopped
  spinach, thawed and drained
2 c. shredded mozzarella cheese,
  divided
1 c. cooked ham, diced
2 c. cooked chicken, shredded
15-oz. container ricotta cheese
1/2 c. grated Parmesan cheese
1/2 c. fresh parsley, minced
1-1/2 t. garlic powder
1-1/2 t. onion powder
28-oz. jar Alfredo sauce, divided
12-oz. pkg. jumbo shell pasta,
  cooked
Garnish: fresh parsley and tomato,
  chopped

Mix spinach, 1-1/4 cups mozzarella
cheese, ham, chicken, ricotta cheese,
Parmesan cheese, parsley, garlic and
onion powders together; set aside.
Spread 2 cups Alfredo sauce into the
bottom of an ungreased 13"x9" baking
pan; spread one cup sauce into an
ungreased 8"x8" baking pan. Spoon
2 tablespoons filling into each pasta
shell; arrange shells in a single layer
in both pans on top of sauce. Bake,
uncovered, at 350 degrees for 30 to
35 minutes; sprinkle with remaining
mozzarella cheese. Bake an additional
5 minutes, or until cheese melts.
Garnish with parsley and tomato.
Serves 6 to 8.

Stacy Huntley
League City, TX

Chicken, ham and spinach
fill jumbo shells. Serve
it with a salad and you
have a delicious meal.

# White Maple Fudge

3 c. sugar
5-oz. can evaporated milk
3/4 c. butter
12-oz. pkg. white chocolate chips
7-oz. jar marshmallow creme
1 t. vanilla extract
1 T. maple flavoring
1/2 to 1 c. pecans, chopped
   or halved

In a large saucepan, mix together sugar, evaporated milk and butter over medium heat, stirring constantly. Bring to a full rolling boil; continue stirring constantly at a full boil for 4 minutes. Remove from heat. Stir in white chocolate chips and marshmallow creme; stir in vanilla and maple flavoring. Add chopped pecans, if using, or wait if using pecan halves. Pour warm fudge into a greased 11"x7" baking pan. If using pecan halves, press into top of fudge. Let set for several hours to overnight; cut into squares. Makes 2-1/2 dozen squares.

Dianna Pindell
Wooster, OH

The most scrumptious fudge ever...and oh-so easy to make!

# INDEX

## Appetizers & Snacks

Cheddar-Bacon Balls, 61
Cheese Pops, 16
Game-Time Sausage Bites, 66
Good-for-You Snack, 15
Grandma Paris' Bambinis, 70
Greek Spread, 62
Honey-Lime Wings, 74
Jalapeño Cheese Log, 58
Mac & Cheese Cupcakes, 27
Maple-Topped Sweet Potato Skins, 67
Oven-Fried Chips, 22
Pumpkin Patch Cheese Ball, 79
Ranch Ham & Tortilla Pinwheels, 28
Tex-Mex Mini Chicken Cups, 69
Toasted Ravioli, 60

## Beverages

Autumn Apple Milkshake, 55
Break-of-Day Smoothie, 8
Cranberry Tea, 71
Spicy Citrus Cider, 77
Warm Spiced Milk, 24

## Breakfasts

After-School Doughnuts, 25
Baked Pancakes with Sausage, 11
Bran & Raisin Muffins, 7
Breakfast Burritos, 9
Cinnamon Toast Balls, 14
My Mom's Muffin Doughnuts, 10
Overnight Cherry Oatmeal, 12

## Desserts

Amish Pear Pie, 90
Ben's Pecan Blondies, 95
Cale's Corn Flake Cookies, 30
Caramel Fudge Brownies, 56
Centipede Cakes, 78
Cream-Filled Witches' Hats, 80
Double Crunch Bars, 54
Fancy Caramel Apples, 65
Harvest Apple Cheesecake, 84
Harvest Fruit & Nut Pie, 102
Hauntingly-Good Candy Cake, 75
Honey-Pumpkin Pie, 105
Lucy's Pumpkin-Chocolate Chip Cake, 89
No-Bake Pumpkin-Butterscotch Pie, 45
Oh-So-Easy Peach Cobbler, 39
Orange-Cranberry Cake, 98
Pound Cake S'mores, 50
Quick Lunchbox Cake, 20
Raisin-Filled Cookies, 29
Silver Moons, 76
Spiderweb Cookies, 81
Touchdown Butterscotch Dip, 68
White Maple Fudge, 107

## Mains

Baked Quesadillas, 23
Bowtie Pasta & Veggies, 38
Cheesy Chicken & Noodles, 41
Chicken Nuggets, 26
Cran-Orange Pork Medallions, 87
Garlic Chicken Pizza, 53
Hamburger Crunch, 42

# INDEX

Harvest Home Roast Turkey, 96
Herb Garden Turkey Breast, 82
Homemade Turkey Pot Pie, 88
Homestyle Beef Pot Pie, 104
Honey-Pecan Chicken, 103
Italian Chicken Pie, 46
Kielbasa Mac & Cheese, 36
Maple Pot Roast, 92
Over-Stuffed Shells, 106
Pork Chops with Apple Stuffing, 44
Ravioli Taco Bake, 31
Taco Stacks, 57
Teresa's Potato Chip Fish, 51

## Salads

ABC Salad, 37
Kids' Favorite Fruit Salad, 13
Swampwater Dressing, 73
Thumbs-Up Cornbread Salad, 35

## Sandwiches & Breads

A Pocket Full of Pizza, 17
BBQ Turkey Sandwiches, 63
Cheesy Garlic Rolls, 100
Colossal Hero Sandwich, 59
Mini Turkey-Berry Bites, 18

PB & Berries, 21
Red Pepper Muffins, 32
Sweet-and-Sauerkraut Brats, 48

## Sides

Acorn Squash Fruit Cups, 83
Apricot-Glazed Carrots, 47
Chestnut Stuffing, 93
Corn Sesame Sauté, 49
Fresh Cranberry Relish, 86
Green Bean Bundles, 97
Loaded Mashed Potato Casserole, 94
Mom's Caramel Sweet Potatoes, 101
Parmesan Zucchini Sticks, 34
Scalloped Apples, 52
Slow-Simmered Baked Beans, 40
Tangy Corn Casserole, 99
Zucchini Patties, 72

## Soups

ABC Chicken Soup, 19
Carol's Creamy Tomato Soup, 43
Finnish Sweet Potato Soup, 91
Ham & Potato Chowder, 85
Pumpkin Chowder, 64
Slow-Cooker Sweet Potato Chili, 33

# Our Story

Back in 1984, we were next-door neighbors raising our families in the little town of Delaware, Ohio. Two moms with small children, we were looking for a way to do what we loved and stay home with the kids too. We had always shared a love of home cooking and making memories with family & friends and so, after many a conversation over the backyard fence, **Gooseberry Patch** was born.

We put together our first catalog at our kitchen tables, enlisting the help of our loved ones wherever we could. From that very first mailing, we found an immediate connection with many of our customers and it wasn't long before we began receiving letters, photos and recipes from these new friends. In 1992, we put together our very first cookbook, compiled from hundreds of these recipes and, the rest, as they say, is history.

Hard to believe it's been over 25 years since those kitchen-table days! From that original little **Gooseberry Patch** family, we've grown to include an amazing group of creative folks who love cooking, decorating and creating as much as we do. Today, we're best known for our homestyle, family-friendly cookbooks, now recognized as national bestsellers.

Vickie & Jo Ann

One thing's for sure, we couldn't have done it without our friends all across the country. Each year, we're honored to turn thousands of your recipes into our collectible cookbooks. Our hope is that each book captures the stories and heart of all of you who have shared with us. Whether you've been with us since the beginning or are just discovering us, welcome to the **Gooseberry Patch** family!

Visit us online:
# www.gooseberrypatch.com
# 1·800·854·6673

# U.S. to Canadian Recipe Equivalents

## Volume Measurements

| | |
|---|---|
| 1/4 teaspoon | 1 mL |
| 1/2 teaspoon | 2 mL |
| 1 teaspoon | 5 mL |
| 1 tablespoon = 3 teaspoons | 15 mL |
| 2 tablespoons = 1 fluid ounce | 30 mL |
| 1/4 cup | 60 mL |
| 1/3 cup | 75 mL |
| 1/2 cup = 4 fluid ounces | 125 mL |
| 1 cup = 8 fluid ounces | 250 mL |
| 2 cups = 1 pint =16 fluid ounces | 500 mL |
| 4 cups = 1 quart | 1 L |

## Weights

| | |
|---|---|
| 1 ounce | 30 g |
| 4 ounces | 120 g |
| 8 ounces | 225 g |
| 16 ounces = 1 pound | 450 g |

## Oven Temperatures

| | |
|---|---|
| 300° F | 150° C |
| 325° F | 160° C |
| 350° F | 180° C |
| 375° F | 190° C |
| 400° F | 200° C |
| 450° F | 230° C |

## Baking Pan Sizes

*Square*

| | |
|---|---|
| 8x8x2 inches | 2 L = 20x20x5 cm |
| 9x9x2 inches | 2.5 L = 23x23x5 cm |

*Rectangular*

| | |
|---|---|
| 13x9x2 inches | 3.5 L = 33x23x5 cm |

*Loaf*

| | |
|---|---|
| 9x5x3 inches | 2 L = 23x13x7 cm |

*Round*

| | |
|---|---|
| 8x1-1/2 inches | 1.2 L = 20x4 cm |
| 9x1-1/2 inches | 1.5 L = 23x4 cm |

# Recipe Abbreviations

| | |
|---|---|
| t. = teaspoon | ltr. = liter |
| T. = tablespoon | oz. = ounce |
| c. = cup | lb. = pound |
| pt. = pint | doz. = dozen |
| qt. = quart | pkg. = package |
| gal. = gallon | env. = envelope |

# Kitchen Measurements

A pinch = 1/8 tablespoon
3 teaspoons = 1 tablespoon
2 tablespoons = 1/8 cup
4 tablespoons = 1/4 cup
8 tablespoons = 1/2 cup
16 tablespoons = 1 cup
2 cups = 1 pint
4 cups = 1 quart
4 quarts = 1 gallon

1 fluid ounce = 2 tablespoons
4 fluid ounces = 1/2 cup
8 fluid ounces = 1 cup
16 fluid ounces = 1 pint
32 fluid ounces = 1 quart
16 ounces net weight = 1 pound